Original title:

Who Needs Meaning When You Have Cats?

Author: Nora Sinclair

ISBN HARDBACK: 978-1-80566-127-6

ISBN PAPERBACK: 978-1-80566-422-2

Life's Delightful Distractions

Furry paws upon the floor,
Chasing dust with all their lore.
A glimmering toy, a sudden leap,
Endless laughter, joy runs deep.

In sunlit patches, they repose,
Dreaming dreams in lazy doze.
With swishes, twitches, playful fights,
They are the kings of cozy nights.

Serene Shadows and Stripes

Whiskers twitching in the sun,
Like tiny ninjas on the run.
Stealthy steps on silent paws,
Creating chaos without flaws.

A patch of light, they claim with glee,
Their royal throne, for all to see.
In the serenade of a cat's purr,
Life's worries fade; there's no deter.

The Joy of a Spinning Tail

Round and round, it whips and sways,
A tiny dancer in playful ways.
With every twist, a chuckle flies,
Oh, the joy that never dies!

A flick, a swish, it draws us in,
In each wild chase, the giggles begin.
Who needs a plan when tails are near?
A simple life; what's there to fear?

Meow Musings

Pondering life from window's edge,
Dramatic stares, a feline pledge.
What thoughts reside in that fluffy head?
Mysteries abound in the joy they've spread.

In twinkling eyes, the world unfolds,
Every moment, a story told.
A gentle purr, a playful smack,
In cat's embrace, there's nothing we lack.

Snuggles of Serenity

In sunbeams warm, they softly nap,
A furry foot hangs, caught in a trap.
With twitches and dreams, they purr away,
As we wonder what they think, all day.

A master of chaos, a fuzzy ball,
They reign supreme in the hallway hall.
Chasing shadows, they dart and dive,
With leaps that make us feel alive.

On laps they land, an unexpected weight,
Reading our minds, they know it's fate.
They claim the space that we hold dear,
In their kingdom, there's naught to fear.

When breakfast calls, they lead the charge,
Determined and fierce, making life large.
With a flick of a tail, they win the day,
A cat's antics, the grandest ballet.

The Purrfect Escape into Absurdity

A leap from the shelf, a clamber and bound,
They plot and scheme, in silence profound.
With a flick of their ear, they stake their claim,
In the wild world of play, they rampage and tame.

A cardboard box turns into a throne,
Where every knickknack is claimed as their own.
With eyes that gleam like the stars at night,
They conquer the room, a magnificent sight.

They wrestle with shadows, they battle with dust,
In their universe grand, it's all a must.
Each leap an adventure, each pounce a spree,
The world is their stage; it's chaos, you see.

And when the clock strikes the hour to rest,
They curl like a question mark, cozy and blessed.
In this puzzling world, they reign supreme,
Chasing the moon in their whimsical dream.

Feline Curiosity and Serene Reflection

A whisker twist, a curious gaze,
They ponder life in silly ways.
Chasing shadows, plotting schemes,
In sunlit naps, they live their dreams.

With paws that tiptoe through the air,
Exploring corners without a care.
They strut like royalty on the floor,
Claiming spaces, always wanting more.

Paws and Effortless Truths

A pounce, a leap, the perfect catch,
A ball of yarn, their favorite match.
They strut in circles, then collapse,
You can't deny their unmatched laps.

With every purr, they tell a tale,
Of lazy days where no one fails.
The sun is theirs, just watch them sprawl,
In feline logic, they conquer all.

Laughter in the Fur

A tumble here, a tumble there,
With mischief twinkling in the air.
They chase their tails, what fun to see,
Oh, the joy of pure felinity!

A meow, a purr, a gentle head butt,
At comedy hour, they strut their stuff.
Cuddles and chaos, such a delight,
In kitty antics, the world feels right.

Cat Wonders and Wandering Minds

They scale the shelves, a daring feat,
As if on a mission, oh so sweet.
In cardboard boxes, they fit just right,
The world's in their paws, what a sight!

They dream of mice, and birds, and more,
With sleepy eyes, they softly snore.
Philosophers in fur coats stroll,
In their little hearts, the world is whole.

The Melody in the Mew

A serenade in purring tones,
Each meow a note, each stretch, a moan.
To chase the sun, they flawlessly race,
While dreams of fish dance on their face.

In the quiet hours, they plot and scheme,
On paper piles where they dare to dream.
With every leap, a laugh is near,
Life's a song when fur is here.

Puzzles in Purrs

Oh, the enigma of the twisting tail,
A riddle wrapped in a fuzzy veil.
With every purr, they weave a charm,
No human mind can sound the alarm.

They hide in boxes, they pop out with glee,
Turning common spaces into a grande spree.
Each nap a challenge, each stretch a clue,
Who needs a puzzle when I've got you?

Shadows of Softness and Silliness

In shadows they prance, with stealthy grace,
Like little ninjas in a playful race.
A flick of the tail, a leap in the air,
They make the mundane feel debonair.

Caught in sunbeams, they dream without care,
A pillow for seconds, their throne, a rare fare.
With whims of a child, and spirits so spry,
Life's a laugh when you let out a sigh.

Fluffy Philosophers in Action

On high perches, in deep thought they sit,
Contemplating whether to nap or to quit.
With paws crossed gently, they ponder the day,
Is this bowl tasty, or just a cliche?

They muse on the wonders of yarn and a string,
Debating with wisdom on each tiny thing.
Their lectures are loud, their conclusions absurd,
But life's golden truths lie in every word.

Purrs of Perspective

A cat sprawled wide on a sunny mat,
With dreams of chasing a lazy rat.
Why stress about life and its messy ways,
When you can nap all night and laze all day?

The world rushes by in a frantic blur,
While they sit in the sun without a stir.
No care for the clock, nor ticking hands,
Just purr-filled moments in cozy lands.

Cotton Clouds of Comfort

Soft as a whisper, a bundle of fur,
Reclines like a king, with no need to purr.
Fluffy clouds on my lap, oh what a sight,
Turning mundane days into pure delight.

They chase their tails with a graceful twirl,
In a world of chaos, they give it a whirl.
A leap, a bound, then a nap on my shoes,
Reminding me daily to take time to snooze.

Playful Paws on the Path

Tiny paws dance on the wooden floor,
Chasing shadows, then wanting more.
Who needs a reason to frolic and play?
When each day's a circus in the cat ballet.

With winks and meows, they steal your heart,
From these furry jesters, it's hard to part.
Life's nonsense wrapped in a whiskered grin,
The joy they bring makes the world spin.

Couch Dwellers' Philosophy

Philosophers lounging with fur coats on,
Debating the merits of the softest lawn.
Their logic is simple: nap, eat, then chase,
Content in their kingdom, they rule with grace.

With a twitch of a tail, they ponder it all,
Should it be a nap or a spontaneous roll?
In the grand scheme of things, they've got it down,
As couch potato kings in their fuzzy crown.

When Whiskers Whisper Secrets

In the quiet of night, they creep,
Soft paws dancing, secrets to keep.
With eyes that glimmer like stars above,
They plot their mischief, those bundles of love.

A twitch of the tail, a flick of the ear,
Whiskers quiver in whispers we hear.
They'll swat at the shadows, then leap with glee,
Masters of chaos, oh can't you see?

The Delight of Daily Antics

Every morning the circus begins,
As they chase their tails and nibble on sins.
A leap, a tumble, a pirouette tight,
Feline gymnastics at dawn's early light.

The laughingly loud pounce on a shoe,
Caught in their act, what's a owner to do?
They summon a storm with a flick of their paw,
In their world of fun, we can only guffaw.

Furry Companions and the Joy of Being

With fur like clouds and eyes like gems,
They cuddle so close, my fuzzy friends.
Each snooze a treasure, every purr a song,
In the presence of cats, nothing feels wrong.

They'll knock things over, a playful tease,
Life's little messes they handle with ease.
With a blink and a stretch, then off like a dart,
These furry companions have captured my heart.

The Poetry of Purring Hearts

In the lap of the day, they softly purr,
Like nature's own tune, that gentle stir.
With a cheeky paw and a little meow,
They bring a chuckle with each little vow.

Sunbeams become their personal stage,
Each quirky pose, their joyful page.
As they nap and frolic, it's clear to see,
The poet in fur gives life's glee to me.

Happiness Curled in a Cozy Ball

In sunbeam spots, they take their ease,
Fluffy bodies, masters of tease.
Chasing shadows, pouncing around,
Happiness found where warmth is found.

A nap is their favorite delight,
Dreams of fish and daring flight.
With a twitch of a paw, they play,
Joyful moments, come what may.

Catnip Dreams and Midnight Prances

Whiskers twitching, eyes aglow,
Chasing mischief, putting on a show.
Leaping high, then landing soft,
Paws in the air, like clouds aloft.

Nightly capers under the moon,
They dance and prance, a furry tune.
Silly antics, the world's their stage,
Filled with laughter, turning the page.

Tails Telling Tales of Joy

Tails flick and swish, a lively dance,
Every movement, a chance to prance.
Stories whispered in purrs and meows,
Joyful secrets, we take our bows.

A gentle nudge, a playful bite,
They reign supreme in the soft night light.
With each whisker, a tale unfolds,
In their world, pure joy beholds.

Paws on the Path to Contentment

Exploring nooks with curious glee,
Paws on a journey, wild and free.
Socks become prey, a mighty foe,
Every corner, a new show to grow.

With a stretch and a yawn, they claim their space,
Life's little pleasures, a fur-lined embrace.
Chasing dust motes, under the sun,
In their company, we've already won.

Living in the Present with Paws

A fleeting glance, a twitching tail,
Each moment's gold, no need to bail.
A napping prince on sunlit ground,
In this soft world, pure joy is found.

Chasing dust motes in the air,
Serious thoughts, they do not care.
With silly leaps, and gentle grace,
The present's where they find their place.

Purring Amidst Life's Mysteries

Wisdom wrapped in fur-like silt,
With every purr, life's stress is spilt.
Untangling strings of fate and thread,
On purring pillows, dreams are spread.

Mysterious stares from moonlit trails,
Beneath the stars, there's laughter's wails.
Paws dance lightly on cosmic beams,
In feline realms, we chase our dreams.

Shadows and Sunbeams: A Feline Tale

In sun-soaked corners, shadows play,
With every leap, they steal the day.
Under the couch, a kingdom reigns,
Where every sound ignites their lanes.

A flick of ear, a stealthy stalk,
They'd win the race in any walk.
Conspiracies in heaps of fluff,
Life's not so serious—enough is enough.

Simplicity Wrapped in Soft Coats

In cozy spots, they take their stand,
Life's complex threads rest in their hand.
Whiskers twitch at the world outside,
As naps and snacks become their ride.

They wander through dreams with joyous ease,
Epiphanies found in playful tease.
With every paw print on the floor,
We discover life is never a bore.

The Charm of Napping Together

Whiskers twitch in dreamland's glow,
Purring softly, hearts in tow.
A sunbeam shines on cozy cats,
Who needs more when this is that?

Tails curled tight in sweet embrace,
Time stands still in this warm space.
With every snore, the world seems right,
In cushy dreams, we share our night.

Furry Footprints on the Road of Joy

Tiny paw prints on the floor,
Each one whispers 'give me more!'
Chasing shadows, a playful spree,
Joy is found in pure kitty glee.

A leap, a bound, they dash and play,
Turning mundane hours bright as day.
With every pounce, they bring such cheer,
Furry footprints, our joy is near.

Cats: Guardians of the Everyday

Sitting tall, watching the world,
Eyes like jewels, fur unfurled.
Stationed firm in every nook,
They guard our hearts without a look.

Stealthy ninjas of the night,
Pounce and purr, oh what delight!
Every bite of food must pass,
For cats reign supreme in every class.

The Magic of Playtime Pounces

With a flick, they bound and dart,
Chasing strings with feline art.
A crinkly toy fluffs up their flight,
Each leap a spark of pure delight.

Claws outstretched, they stalk the air,
As if the world is theirs to share.
With laughter ringing soft and clear,
Playtime magic draws us near.

Purring Through the Paradox

In a world of chaos, they reign supreme,
Asleep on our laps, living the dream.
Chasing shadows, with no care,
Philosophers wrapped in a furry lair.

They grasp the truth, we scramble to find,
With the flick of a tail, they'd leave us behind.
Naps hold more wisdom than books on a shelf,
A meow of coyness, their thoughts kept to self.

Freedom in Fur

Through open windows, they boldly roam,
Claiming the world, each cushion, each home.
Life is a playground, they run and they leap,
While we trudge along, counting sheep.

Boxes are castles, a throne in the sun,
Every crinkle, a treasure, a journey begun.
With a lollipop sway, they conquer the day,
For them, every moment is a playful ballet.

Feline Flâneur

Strolling through halls like they own the place,
A sideways glance hides a cheeky grace.
Paws soft as whispers, they glide with flair,
Pretending indifference, we know they care.

Critiques of our lives with a disdainful stare,
On the windowsill judging the passing air.
With each little pounce, they're setting the stage,
For a comedy show that defies any age.

The Untamed Mind of Tails

A flick of the tail, it speaks volumes loud,
Echoing plans to break through the crowd.
From tippy-toes stealthy to leaping so high,
Every leap is a question, a wink of the eye.

In this kingdom of fluff, wisdoms are shared,
With each little pounce, we're all unprepared.
They plot the takeover, while we simply laugh,
In their furry dominion, they lead the staff.

Whiskered Whims of a Carefree Soul

With paws that prance and tails that sway,
A fuzzy overlord leads the way.
Chasing dust motes in the sun,
Life's golden moments, just for fun.

A leap of faith on the nearest chair,
A daring dreamer with fluffy flair.
Silly antics in every room,
A rolling ball sparks feline zoom.

Each nap they take from noon till three,
A throne of comfort, that's where they'll be.
Pillow fort under the coffee table,
No grand adventures, but they're quite able.

Happiness found in a cardboard box,
No need for treasures, just fluffed-up socks.
With every purr and every scratch,
Life's profound, but they're a perfect match.

Purrs Over Purpose

In the morning light with a sleepy yawn,
A furry creature greets the dawn.
With a purr that echoes like a song,
No purpose needed where they belong.

Socks are toys and chairs the stage,
Each playful moment, a scripted page.
A leap and spin, a twist of fate,
In their wild world, time won't wait.

They plot and scheme with glittering eyes,
While pondering thoughts of ultimate fries.
When life gets heavy, just watch them play,
As wisdom is found in their silly ways.

Who needs a plan, a schedule or goal?
When nap time's the answer to every soul.
With laughter and joy, they fill the air,
Their fuzzy smiles, a remedy rare.

Feline Revelations in Sunlit Naps

A cat curls up in the warm sunbeam,
Chasing sweet visions in a daydream.
With paws tucked in and whiskers askew,
They're masters of art in their cozy brew.

A twitch of a tail and a soft little snore,
With dreams of fishies and open doors.
Life's a canvas of naps and plays,
They find joy in the simplest ways.

In dappled light, their secrets unfold,
With every stretch, stories are told.
Is it catnip or magic that fuels their fire?
In sunlit naps, they never tire.

Mischief brews with every new glance,
Caught in the act of a ridiculous dance.
From puzzled humans to feline surprise,
Such hilarity hides behind their wise eyes.

The Language of Cat Stares

In stillness, a gaze cuts through the air,
A look of disdain or an offer to share?
With just one blink, it's all understood,
A plan, a plot, or a quest for food.

Yet when they curl beside you in bliss,
That lingering gaze feels like a kiss.
Pleading eyes for snacks at dawn,
In their world, responsibility is just a con.

The way they stare when you're on your phone,
As if to say, 'Hey, you're not alone!'
With every glance, they weave a spell,
A silent language that speaks so well.

So while you ponder your purpose and goals,
A saucer of milk fills up their holes.
In every stare, they send out a cue,
It's time to laugh, there's fun to pursue.

Cats: The True Masters of Zen

In sunlit spots they lie, serene,
With paws tucked in, the perfect scene.
Chasing shadows on the wall,
In blissful naps, they heed the call.

Buddha would envy their tranquil grace,
As they stretch out in a cozy space.
With just a purr, they calm the mind,
Such wisdom in fur, so hard to find!

They watch the world with knowing eyes,
Plotting mischief, oh what a surprise!
And when they leap with boundless glee,
They teach us joy, so wild and free.

With every slinky, gentle sway,
They remind us to seize the day.
In every whisker, wisdom grows,
These feline sages, our true pros.

Untamed Joy in Every Meow

Each little meow, a burst of cheer,
A tiny roar, nothing to fear.
With swats at ghosts that just can't be,
Their laughter echoes—a symphony!

From pouncing paws to mischief spun,
Every day feels like a wild run.
On towers of pillows, they reign supreme,
A kingdom built on whimsy and dream.

In cardboard boxes, their thrones await,
They leap like ninjas with stealthy gait.
Wreaking havoc with fluffy finesse,
Their joyous antics, we must confess.

So raise a toast to their playful ways,
For every meow brightens our days.
In the world of cats, let fun abound,
Endless laughter is always found!

In the Company of Comfort

Curled in a ball, warm as could be,
Feline hugs bring tranquility.
With gentle purrs like softest streams,
They lull our minds into sweet dreams.

A twitch of a tail, a playful glance,
In cozy corners, they love to dance.
With every cuddle, worries cease,
In the arms of cats, we find our peace.

When life gets tough, their presence near,
Soothes the soul and calms the fear.
In the company of fluff and bliss,
We find the joy in a whiskered kiss.

So here's to cats, our snuggly friends,
Their love and laughter never ends.
In their soft world, we often roam,
With every purr, they bring us home.

Tales from the Lap of Abandon

Stories unfold with each cuddly nap,
In the warm embrace of a feline lap.
They dream of fish and faraway lands,
With graceful paws, they make their plans.

Their world is rich, with yarns to spin,
Every creak and crack invites a grin.
They ponder deeply, yet so carefree,
Foreseeing greatness in a sunny spree.

Napping heroes with hearts so bold,
Guardians of secrets, both new and old.
In their gentle sway, we lose the race,
Finding life's joy in every space.

With tales of wonder by the fireside,
We share their laughter, hearts open wide.
In their plush realm, time slips away,
As we cherish each paw-filled day.

Cuddles and Cosmic Queries

Fuzzy creatures on a throne,
They rule the realm, yet sleep alone.
With curious eyes, they gaze up high,
While pondering the truth of why.

Paws in the air, they take a leap,
Chasing shadows, then back to sleep.
Questions arise in playful mews,
What do they think, what do they choose?

Napping in sunbeams, dreams unfold,
Their silent wisdom, a story told.
We question life, they catch a breeze,
In their world, it's all just tease.

With every pounce and whisker twitch,
They find the joy, ditching the hitch.
No need for meaning, just purrs and play,
In their feline realm, it's always a day.

Velvet Claws and Quiet Reflections

Soft as a cloud, paws like velvet,
Curled in content, no need to fret.
Philosophers in paws, they sit so still,
As their minds dance to an unspoken thrill.

Nibbling dreams in the afternoon sun,
The great debate is just for fun.
A flick of the tail, a dignified stare,
Life's little puzzles fill the air.

They ponder food, a world so vast,
Reflecting on meals that go so fast.
As shadows creep, they come alive,
In their kingdom of whims, all thoughts thrive.

Each cuddle shared, a priceless find,
Their playful antics are simply divine.
With velvet claws, they tread the line,
Meaning's absurdity in every twine.

The Leisurely Pursuit of Purring

Time ticks slow while they bask and curl,
In sunlit spots, they dance and twirl.
A purr escapes, like music sweet,
In every moment, a purrfect beat.

Toy mice scatter, a wild pursuit,
Chasing with finesse, oh what a hoot!
But what they catch is just a fluff,
In their eyes, that's more than enough.

Food is an art form, a culinary quest,
Every bowl served, they're surely blessed.
They rise and shine with sleepy grace,
For every meal is a royal embrace.

As twilight falls, they serenade the night,
With whispered dreams, they take flight.
In the art of lounging, they are the kings,
In their fuzzy lives, it's laughter that sings.

Claw-some Contradictions

Masters of chaos, yet full of ease,
They climb our curtains, bring us to knees.
One minute sweet, the next a wild show,
These furry enigmas, what do we know?

They reign on our laps, then dash for a toy,
Such unexpected antics that bring us joy.
Life's mysteries seem simple and clear,
When you watch a cat leap, you can't help but cheer.

In quiet moments, they ponder their fate,
As we ponder our lives, they lie there sedate.
They teach us to laugh, to love, to lose track,
In the world of a cat, there's no looking back.

A riddle wrapped up in whiskers and fluff,
Their love is unconditional, fierce, and tough.
So here's to the cats, our joy and our thrill,
In their claw-some ways, life seems to stand still.

Embracing Chaos with Claws

A leap here, a pounce there, oh what a sight,
As fur flies around, bringing pure delight.
Knocking over cups with a flick of a tail,
Every day's a circus, never a dull tale.

Chasing shadows, trapped in a box,
Plotting world domination from cozy socks.
Purring loudly, making the bed their throne,
In a kingdom of chaos, they rule alone.

The laundry's a jungle, the crumbs are the prey,
They bat at strips of paper like it's their play.
Creating mischief with a simple meow,
In this chaotic life, they take their bow.

So here's to the rulers of our crazy days,
With laughter and joy in their playful ways.
Embracing the mess, we'll never complain,
With these furry companions, there's never a strain.

The Universe in Their Eyes

Two tiny galaxies in curious orbs,
As they gaze into space, their wisdom absorbs.
With every slow blink, they ponder the stars,
While plotting their next chase, unbothered by scars.

What mysteries lie in a furry embrace?
Time stops, and the world is a quiet place.
They dream of the cosmos, with naps in between,
In a universe ruled by whiskers and sheen.

Each meow is profound, like a sage's decree,
As they saunter through life, happy and free.
Tales of adventure curl up by their side,
In a whimsical world where pure magic resides.

So let's raise a glass to these sages of fluff,
Who turn moments mundane into diamond-studded stuff.
With the universe shining in their cat-sized eyes,
Life's questions seem silly and laughter just flies.

Whiskers on Whimsy

In a world of whimsy, they prance and play,
With paws full of mischief and joy every day.
A flutter of feathers, the rustle of grass,
Their laughter echoing, as moments fly past.

They twirl with the curtains, a dance of delight,
Each flip of their tail brings a giggle so bright.
Pouncing on sunshine, a game of hot chase,
With every tumble, they conquer their space.

The sound of their purr is a whimsical tune,
As they stretch like a ship against a bright moon.
Life's tending to chaos, but they take it with glee,
In the realm of their hearts, they hold the key.

So let's cherish these jesters who rise with the dawn,
With leaps into laughter and yawns that are drawn.
In a land filled with whiskers and moments so silly,
Life's a merry-go-round, and joy rolls in freely.

Feline Philosophy

In the world of the wise, they rule with a paw,
Curl up with a philosopher and hear their 'awe'.
Life's simple pleasures, a sunbeam to lounge,
As they ponder the cosmos from a velvet-bound couch.

With seriousness masked by a playful refrain,
They muse on existence while chasing a chain.
A whiff of the breeze is a thought to explore,
In every small moment, they ask for much more.

When caught in a nap, they dream of the chase,
Conquerors at heart in a fuzzy embrace.
The meaning of life wrapped in whiskers and purrs,
Philosophers with tails, in soft little furs.

So let's listen closely to these furry wise friends,
For wisdom may come where the laughter transcends.
In cat-like reflections, we'll find joy displayed,
With feline philosophy, our worries evade.

Cats and Cosmic Curiosities

In a sunbeam, they plot and scheme,
Chasing shadows, lost in a dream.
With a flick of the tail, they rule the land,
While humans just try to understand.

Galactic purring, vibrations so deep,
Local gravity? They just leap.
A universe filled with playful glances,
As cats unfold their nightly romances.

The Solace of a Catnap

Curled in a ball, with eyes shut tight,
Dreaming of tuna, it feels just right.
A gentle snore in the afternoon glow,
Contentment found in a world moving slow.

The couch is their throne, soft and warm,
In fuzzy dreams, there's never a storm.
Time drips away, like a leisurely stream,
While humans rush by, lost in a dream.

Whiskered Zen

On the windowsill, they sit and stare,
Philosophers clad in fur with flair.
Contemplating the meaning of life,
While planning their pounce on unsuspecting strife.

Every whisker's twitch tells a profound tale,
Of stealthy hunts and imaginary trails.
In silence they embody the world's great quest,
Finding joy in the mundane, they are truly blessed.

The Silent Symphony of Meows

A feline concert at the break of dawn,
With melodies soft, like a silky lawn.
Each meow a note in the harmony bright,
As cats serenade the waking light.

A grand overture with paws on the floor,
Each whisker vibrating with tales galore.
An unspoken language we're yet to decode,
But laughter erupts in this furry abode.

The Art of Cat Naps

In sunlit spots they curl and dream,
Paws twitching in a silent scheme.
A nap so deep, they barely breathe,
Drifting softly, hearts reprieved.

They wake with stretches, yawns galore,
Then off to chase that phantom spore.
On feathered beds, their reigns are grand,
A life of leisure, oh so planned.

A blink, a blink, and they are gone,
Across the room, they stealthily bawn.
With every pounce and playful bounce,
They redefine the art of sounds.

In every fluff-stuffed, cozy nook,
Lie tales of naps in storybooks.
With hearts so light, they snooze away,
While worldly troubles fade and sway.

Mischief and Meaninglessness

A swish of tails, a sudden leap,
The goldfish bowl now in a heap!
With tiny paws, they prowl the night,
In realms of chaos, all feels right.

Wreaking havoc, they're quite the thieves,
Unraveling yarn like fallen leaves.
In pointless games, they take their glee,
Oh, what a life, so wild and free!

They strut like kings upon the chair,
With no care made for what is fair.
They steal our hearts, our socks, and dreams,
While we pretend it's what it seems.

And in their laughter, pure delight,
We find our joy, that sweet respite.
For in their world of wanders wild,
Meaning's lost, but joy's a child.

Beneath the Feline Spell

Eyes like moons and hearts of gold,
In their gaze, the world unfolds.
With every purr, we're lulled to peace,
As all our worries seem to cease.

They rule the couch, the bed, the chair,
Occupying space without a care.
Through winding paths of dreams they stroll,
Each twitch a tiny, sweet parole.

In snuggles tight, they plant their claim,
And we forget our mundane game.
With silly quirks that make us laugh,
Life becomes a joyful craft.

Their whims bring laughter, soft and loud,
We dance with joy, we're feeling proud.
For in their spell, we find our way,
No need for meaning, just their play.

Velvet Whims and Wandering Thoughts

On velvet paws, they plot and scheme,
A world to conquer, or so it seems.
With fancy leaps and lazy sighs,
They catch our hearts, oh how they rise!

Wandering thoughts, they mimic well,
As shadows play, they weave their spell.
Through kitchens, halls, they make their rounds,
Ignoring all the worldly bounds.

For every mischief, a little smile,
In warmth and fluff, we find our style.
With antics grand, and whiskers bright,
They fill our days with pure delight.

So let the world spin on its axis,
As we indulge in feline praxis.
For joy is found in purrs and climbs,
In this pure chaos, there's no need for rhymes.

Tails of Ease

Chasing shadows, naps on the floor,
Laziness is a feline lore.
A purrfect life without a care,
Sunbeam throne, without a share.

Kitchen raids for a treat or two,
With stealthy moves, they slink and skew.
Forget the mail, it's all a game,
Yet still, they charm us all the same.

A swish of tails, a blink of green,
An unexpected, regal scene.
We laugh at their antics, day and night,
In their fuzzy reign, everything's right.

So let them rule, our furry jest,
In these simple moments, we are blessed.
With every leap and playful tease,
Life's true joy is found in these.

Clueless in Catland

A sudden leap, the couch a stage,
Cats in chaos, like wild rampage.
Tangled yarn and a feathered toy,
Endless antics, a purring joy.

They plot and plan with a serious glare,
Only to end up in a curled-up square.
The world's a puzzle, they search and paw,
In their kingdom, we're just in awe.

Strange noises from an empty box,
The unseen threat of mysterious socks.
With every gaze, they seem to say,
"Why isn't this mundane fun today?"

With whisker twitches and playful bites,
They usher in our silly nights.
In a world of blissfully clueless plays,
Our hearts are stolen in endless ways.

Catnip Dreams and Daydreams

A sprinkle of joy in a patch of green,
A dreamy cat lost in the scene.
Rolling, rolling, in scents so sweet,
In catnip dreams, they find their beat.

Paws in the air, with no shame to spare,
They rule their world without a care.
Chasing whispers only they can hear,
In their daydreams, they conquer fear.

With grand delusions of mice on the prowl,
They leap with grace, then softly howl.
In this fantasy, it's always spring,
A realm where cats are the perfect king.

So let them chase that mystical flair,
In their laughable quests, we find our air.
For in their frolic of whimsy and glee,
We join the jest, forever carefree.

Wistful Whiskers

With whiskered faces and dreamy sighs,
They ponder life through narrowed eyes.
Perched high above on lofty towers,
They rule their realms for endless hours.

A fleeting thought in a sunbeam's light,
Should they leap down, or stay in flight?
Curled in corners, lost in thought,
Of fishy dreams they bravely sought.

Their gaze is wise, their actions meek,
In every pounce, adventure peaks.
Yet snugly wrapped in cozy folds,
They tell the stories that never get old.

For every nap and gentle purr,
Life's sweet moments, they prefer.
With wistful whiskers, they softly scheme,
In a world that's just one big catnap dream.

Soft Pawed Epiphanies

In the sunbeam, they take their throne,
Feline rulers, we're not alone.
Life's great mysteries, they do ignore,
Chasing shadows, then wanting more.

With a twitch of a tail, they reel us in,
A fleeting moment, in a world of sin.
Nap time declared, all plans on hold,
Their soft purrs, much more than gold.

Litter box prophets, wise beyond years,
Judging us softly, despite our fears.
Dreaming of fish, while naught but a snack,
In their kingdom of comfort, we lose track.

Furballs remind us, it's all just play,
A life full of wonders, yet light as a ray.
Let go of deep thoughts, release that tense knot,
For wisdom is found where the sunlight is hot.

Claws on Curiosities

Little furry detectives, on a grand quest,
Exploring the world, they know what's best.
Unraveling secrets with each tiny paw,
Finding lost trinkets, they leave us in awe.

On a window ledge, they gaze and they plot,
An unknown bug, a hand that's forgot.
They leap and they bound, in supreme acrobatics,
Our worries forgotten; they're the true theatrics.

Boxes are portals, imaginative doors,
A cat in a box is a reason for roars.
Crammed into corners, they shed all their woes,
Life's a grand stage, and they steal the show!

Meowing at moons, planning nighttime schemes,
Chasing the breeze, in celestial dreams.
With every soft pounce, a new joy will spark,
Curiosity thrives in the warmth of the dark.

Whiskered Wonders

With a twitch of their whiskers, they steal our hearts,
Charmers of chaos, with sneaky sly arts.
A leap from the shelf, a cat on the spree,
In the dance of their whims, we're happy to be.

Magicians of mischief, with each little prance,
They pull us in close for a silly romance.
Fuzzy detectives in the world of delight,
Every soft paw print makes life feel just right.

Dreams are their playground, the night's their domain,
Chasing elusive thoughts like a playful hurricane.
We laugh out loud at their curious ways,
In a world turned upside down, they astound and amaze.

Gentle purring lullabies soothe our own fears,
Each nuzzle a treasure; they know all our tears.
In their presence, all worries seem terse,
We find all our meaning in this playful verse.

Purring Through Existence

In a sunny patch, a sweet nap begins,
Time flows slower, as the purring spins.
A tiny universe in a blink and a purr,
They teach us to savor, to live with a stir.

Every chase of a toy, a lesson so grand,
To explore with abandon, with no thought, just stand.
Life's little subtleties caught in their gaze,
We smile as they teach us to drift in a daze.

With a flick of a tail, they say it's okay,
To let go of worries, to dance and to play.
Home's where the cat is, that much is clear,
With laughter and purring, we cast out our fear.

For every soft moment, a treasure unfolds,
In the heart of their chaos, true joy it holds.
No need for deep meanings in the lives that we lead,
Just purring companions, fulfilling our need.

Feline Escapades of Thought

In sunbeams stretched upon the floor,
A pondering cat can't help but snore.
Thoughts of fish and mice all day,
Chasing dreams in a furry ballet.

The curtain sways, a mystery hid,
Oh, could it be a ghostly kid?
Eyes squint wide at thumping sounds,
A jumping shadow, it rebounds.

Each box a world, each lap a throne,
With every purr, affection is shown.
Why chase a job or anxious schemes,
When napping's the heart of all good dreams?

Between the snacks and playful leaps,
Is all sentient thought just catnaps in heaps?
To ponder meaning while they preen,
Is a question best left to the feline queen.

Tranquil Tails and Timeless Questions

A tail flick here, a twitching ear,
In moments so calm, who needs career?
With each soft purr and cozy sprawls,
Why chase significance when kitty calls?

They nap in blankets, a plush retreat,
While we sit puzzled at life's heartbeat.
One paw extended, they stretch and sigh,
A feline's zen is quite the high.

Prowling dreams of tuna cans,
Or plotting games with cardboard plans,
Timeless questions of life's design,
Fade away with their catnip shine.

Each furry friend is a brush of glee,
Teaching hearts to flit and flee.
In the world of whiskers and purring prose,
Fun is found where the feline goes.

Serendipitous Snuggles

Under the table, a fuzzy heap,
Grateful for moments, we laugh and leap.
In cuddled chaos, the world takes pause,
Who needs a reason? Just take a cause!

Each gentle knead is a soft reply,
While I ponder the meaning, oh, my oh my!
Is it a job or a feline's ruse,
To take all my time while they snooze?

With whiskers twitching, they steal my breath,
Life's mysteries fade, who cares 'bout death?
Snuggles and purrs, a delightful mess,
Is this the secret to pure happiness?

From couch to lap, they're never far,
In their fuzzy lives, we're all a star.
Finding humor in fur and whiskers,
Our hearts are light, our worries whiskers.

The Tail End of It All

Chasing tails and tangled yarn,
In this furry realm, no one's worn.
A leap, a bound, they own the floor,
As I ponder purpose, they seek out more.

From feline heights, they rule the space,
Conquering thoughts with fierce grace.
With each little scratch, nothing feels wrong,
Who needs life's answers when there's a song?

The dinner bell rings, their ears perk high,
While I sit here with a questioning sigh.
They feast and frolic, it's plain to see,
In their happy chaos, there's joy for me.

So let us bask in soft meows,
Forget the world and its heavy brows.
At the tail end of reason, I sing my quirky call,
A life is most meaningful, beside a cat's sprawl.

Pawsitive Observations

In the sunbeam, they lie and stretch,
Furry philosophers, without a fetch.
Chasing shadows, plotting their game,
Life's little moments, never the same.

A curl of the tail, a twitch of the ear,
Their silly antics, bring so much cheer.
They nap like they've got it all figured out,
As if life's a puzzle, without any doubt.

A leap from the shelf, a startling surprise,
With every flop, a new world to rise.
Sprinkling joy, like glitter on floors,
These fuzzy jesters, the heart always soars.

In a world that's often too serious and grim,
They bat at our troubles, making them dim.
So let's grab some snacks, and enjoy the show,
With cats by our side, we'll never feel low.

Lost in the Litter Box of Life

Life's a maze, I navigate well,
But here comes a cat with a magical spell.
From box to box, they wander and roam,
Leaving their mark, making it home.

Pawprints on papers, a trail of delight,
As they stretch out and claim their birthright.
I ponder existence, they just take a nap,
While I'm left pondering my life's little trap.

A flick of their tail sends me in a spin,
While they swat at the dust, oh where to begin?
Chasing ghostly shadows, in their little quest,
As I chase my worries, forgetting the rest.

So here's to the litter, the joy, and the mess,
With each little meow, they weave happiness.
Life's not a puzzle, when we have these friends,
Just litter-box giggles, and love that extends.

Affection in Every Pounce

A gentle pounce, a soft little landing,
Their love language, so sweet and understanding.
With every cuddle, they weave a soft spell,
In purrs and head bumps, all is well.

They curl in my lap, a warm, furry weight,
No finer companion, it's never too late.
With wide-open eyes, they look up with glee,
In a world of chaos, they find joy for free.

Little paw slips, they tumble and roll,
Every fumble brings giggles, heart, and soul.
They bat at my fingers, their joy fills the air,
Affection in each pounce, life's moments to share.

While profound thoughts may drift in and out,
With every chirp and meow, there's never a doubt.
In their silly charm, I find my delight,
With cats by my side, everything feels right.

Enigmas Wrapped in Fur

Soft little puzzles, wrapped up in fur,
Mysterious beings, they prance and confer.
With a flick of the tail, what do they know?
They're plotting adventures, in a world full of glow.

They stare at the wall, as if seeing beyond,
Whiskers twitching, with secrets to respond.
In their quiet moments, wisdom takes hold,
Yet their silliness never gets old.

The cat on the windowsill, watchful and wise,
Dreaming of kingdoms beneath sunlit skies.
But when the pizza box opens, they spring in a flash,
For love and intrigue, it's the key to their stash.

Wrapped in their riddles, they dance through the day,
With laughter and joy in their own crafty way.
Through moons and the stars, they softly confide,
In the heart of the home, they always reside.

Laughter in Leaps

A cat jumps high, a sight to see,
Chasing shadows, wild, and free.
With a flip and a twist, they land with grace,
In living rooms, they own the space.

Waking at dawn, they pounce and play,
Their antics brightening up the day.
From paper balls to ribbons that fly,
Giggles emerge with every shy try.

Lurking behind skirts, they plot their schemes,
A game of stealth, or so it seems.
Whiskers twitch with mischief aglow,
A furry comedian, stealing the show.

Oh to be wise like our feline friends,
With laughter to share that never ends.
In the warmth of purrs, we find our delight,
A world wrapped in fur, all feels just right.

Cat Tales of Contentment

In sun-soaked spots, they lay so still,
Dreaming of fish, and chasing at will.
With the twitch of a tail, the room comes alive,
A kingdom of cats, where giggles thrive.

They hide in boxes, pop-out with flair,
Surprising the guests, a comical scare.
A leap through the air, a graceful ballet,
Bringing chuckles, brightening the day.

Tail flicking bravely, they strut with pride,
A parade of fluff, nowhere to hide.
Every funny moment a story to share,
In a world of cats, we're light as air.

With a purr and a meow, they call it a night,
Creating a magic, a pure joy-flight.
For in every whisker, and soft little snooze,
Lies a universe built of giggles and hues.

Furry Faith and Frivolity

Waking to purrs, there's magic in store,
Furry friends waiting by the door.
With eyes that glimmer, they plot and scheme,
A daily adventure that's weaved from a dream.

Chasing the sunlight, they dart to and fro,
Behind every corner, their mischief will grow.
A dash through the halls, a wicked delight,
With furry paws padding, they conquer the night.

They perch on the shelves, as if kings and queens,
Regal and ready to feast on their scenes.
Every leap and pounce invites a new laugh,
In a home filled with joy, they're the best half.

With flicks of their tails and soft little mews,
They remind us of fun in our cozy shoes.
In a life filled with fur, there's wisdom, it's true,
Finding joy every day with the ones we love too.

The Silent Wisdom of Cats

In the hush of the night, they prowl and they roam,
Each corner they check feels just like home.
With a flick of a paw, they dance on the edge,
Their quiet approach, a curious hedge.

They know where the sunbeams will cozy and warm,
Finding perfect spots, they weather the storm.
Snoozing so soundly, no worries in sight,
In their world of contentment, all is just right.

With a whisker twitch, they convey all their pride,
Like masters of zen, they glide and they bide.
In moments of laughter, their antics unfold,
Revealing the wisdom that's precious as gold.

So let us be like them, embracing each day,
In the laughter and joy that comes into play.
For in every cat's pause, their secrets align,
In a world filled with fluff, laughter will shine.

The Joyful Mystery of Mews

In shadows they creep, with eyes like stars,
Their antics unfold, like feline memoirs.
A leap and a bound, a flick of the tail,
With every soft purr, we surely can't fail.

They nap in the sun, in the warmest of spots,
Chasing after dreams, while we tie our knots.
A tumble, a roll, they conquer our hearts,
In just a few moments, pure joy never departs.

A toy made of yarn, a string that they chase,
With every sly glance, they quicken our pace.
The mystery's deep, yet so very clear,
Life's better with cats, let's give a loud cheer!

So here's to the meows, the purrs, and the fun,
In a world full of chaos, they're number one.
With whiskers all twitching, and paws that demand,
Each day's an adventure, so grand and unplanned.

Purring Peace and Pet Ideas

There's nothing like purring to calm every soul,
As cats curl up tight, they make us feel whole.
With paws so soft, they knead and they play,
Turning mundane moments into a grand ballet.

Ideas for their fun, a box or a string,
Each little delight makes the heart start to sing.
A leap or a pounce, they're masters of glee,
In their kingdom of laughter, all are set free.

They plan and they plot, little furballs of zest,
With outcomes so silly, we'll never know best.
Oh, how could we measure their whimsical ways,
When every day with them feels like a parade?

So here's to our partners, these fluffy small beasts,
With quirks and with charm, they've captured our feasts.
No deepest of meanings can quite comprehend,
The joy they deliver, our furry best friends.

Whiskers of Wisdom

With whiskers so wise, they ponder and stare,
Our feline companions, they truly don't care.
They lounge with finesse, each paw in the air,
As if they hold secrets that only they share.

They sit on our books, as we try to read,
With looks that say 'Hush! You just missed my lead!'
A swish of their tails, they claim their domain,
In a world of soft chaos, they'll always remain.

They bat at the shadows, a dance so divine,
For every old thought, they bring fresh design.
A meow or a chirp, wisdom often ignored,
May just be the answer we've endlessly searched.

So let them inspire, these quirky old souls,
With every soft purr, they gently console.
In a life full of questions, they whisper it clear:
The answer is simple—just keep them near.

No Purpose, Just Paws

What's the point of order when kittens abound?
With chaos and cuteness, our hearts must confound.
They scatter our papers, they leap and they run,
In a world where they reign, we all have such fun.

The world's their playground, with corners and nooks,
They perch with such flair, like the best storybooks.
A pounce and a dash, each day is absurd,
No purpose required, just love undeterred.

Their footprints are tiny, yet vast is their claim,
In our lives they frolic, with joy that's untamed.
So here's to the moments we spend in delight,
With paws overpurpose, they light up the night.

So laugh at the antics, and share in the fun,
With cats in our lives, we've already won.
Let's toast to their whims, and the joy that they spread,
In a world filled with nonsense, their pawprints are bread.

Cat Thought Corners

In sunlit spots, they plot and scheme,
With glances that burst like a bubble of cream.
Chasing shadows that dance on the wall,
In their world of whimsy, there's room for us all.

Each tangle of yarn, a battle anew,
A pounce on a toaster? Oh yes, they'll skew.
With audacity unmatched and grace divine,
Even the flowers know they're simply a line.

As they nap in the laundry, what wisdom they wield,
Teaching us laughter in every field.
For meaning eludes, but they curl up real tight,
As if to remind us that joy's in the light.

So we sit on the couch, snack in hand,
While they "help" with the paperwork, that's their grandstand.
With a flick of their tails and a yawn oh so wide,
They leave us chortling, our hearts open wide.

Tails of the Unraveled

They leap from the counter with graceful flair,
A ninja attack on the dust in the air.
Their tails tell a tale of mischief and cheer,
Every soft purr whispers, "Come cuddle near."

The feathered toy sways from side to side,
Like a cat with no plan, they're joyfully wide.
With awkward antics and unplanned leaps,
They claim all the cushions, it's plush they must keep.

In the chaos of life, their paws take the lead,
They bring in the sunshine while we tend to weeds.
With naps for a purpose, they teach us to play,
While chaos reigns on this sunny ballet.

So when the world gets a little too loud,
The cat on my lap truly wears a crown.
With goofy charm and a sleepy delight,
Life's meaning comes clear in their feline light.

Purring Into the Unknown

With a swish of the tail, they conquer the night,
As shadows fall gently, their mischief takes flight.
In the corners of dreams, they claim every throne,
Leaving paw prints of laughter wherever they're grown.

They'll chomp on the plant as if it's a feast,
An innocent burglar, a cute little beast.
When they leap from the shelf with a thud and a grin,
The chaos together is where we begin.

As midnight approaches, the purring begins,
A rumbling crescendo as comfort spins.
No need for purpose when soft paws align,
In this dance of delight, we happily dine.

Though the world may be wild with purpose in sight,
The fluff and the fun bring our worries to light.
With cracks in the silence, they playfully purr,
In the depths of each moment, our hearts will incur.

Paws Over Purpose

Slinking through shadows with whiskers all twitch,
A leap and a flop – oh, aren't they a hitch?
While we ponder the stars and the meaning of time,
They're living their best in a world full of mime.

The comfort of fur as the world starts to spin,
Each curl on my lap is a sweet little sin.
No need for big thoughts when a tail flicks just right,
In laughter and purring, the world feels so bright.

Chasing a laser like it's the holy grail,
A determined pursuit of that elusive trail.
In the wreckage of toys, they tumble and play,
With each wobbly stance, they steal breath away.

So as we sit, frowning over what's true,
They dance with delight in a lighthearted brew.
With each sleepy blink and each playful delight,
We find all the meaning in their feline flight.

The Art of Leisure, Cat Edition

In sunny spots they lay, a king's decree,
Their throne is any lap, a sight to see.
With a twitch of a tail, they plot and scheme,
Life's a cozy nap, oh what a dream!

They chase invisible foes, oh such delight,
Pouncing in shadows, in the dead of night.
A laser dot is their ultimate goal,
But none can catch it—ah, the trials of a soul!

Boxes, crumpled paper, the finest toys,
Transforming the mundane into raucous joys.
Every stray sunbeam becomes their stage,
Their antics unfold, breaking all the cage.

With a swish and a purr, they rule the show,
In a realm of fluff, they steal the glow.
While we ponder life, they have it planned,
Embrace the couch, life's just grand!

A World Spun by Soft Paws

Whiskers twitch with mischief, feathered fun,
A world unspooled where the laughter's spun.
Chasing after shadows, reigning with glee,
Each leap, a testament—wild and free!

Dinner time, a regal feast laid down,
Yet it's the box that earns the crown.
Draped on papers, or in a tight curl,
Their charm's a language that makes us twirl.

They conduct symphonies with tiny meows,
As we respond with smiles, and cheerful vows.
Fur on our clothes, a badge we wear,
A token of love, beyond compare!

In their playful kingdom, we find our glee,
Every purr and nudge, a decree to just be.
As we laugh at their whims, our worries fade,
In a world spun by soft paws, love is conveyed.

Furball Philosophy at Dusk

As the sun dips low, a furball's wise gaze,
Sinking in thoughts of snack-time delays.
Curling into corners, meditative sigh,
They ponder the question—why even try?

Chasing their tails with deliberate grace,
How did life become this delightful race?
With a flick of a paw, they declare a truce,
To all human dilemmas, they simply deduce.

Nap, snack, repeat—that's the sacred creed,
Each moment cherished, that's all they need.
Underneath the stars, their hearts do sing,
In a furball's world, curfews are a fling.

So here's to the cats, our furry, wise friends,
With every little purr, they teach us to mend.
They've got it all figured, no need for fuss,
Life's about soft naps—relish this plus!

Serenity Found in a Furry Embrace

Nestled in cushions, a tranquil retreat,
A soft, fuzzy belly, oh, what a treat!
With gentle vibrations, they serenade,
In the warmth of their charm, worries fade.

Each scratch and each rub, a ritual shared,
In their world of whimsy, we're always prepared.
Calm in their presence, the day drifts away,
A whiskered philosopher at play.

Tiny paw prints, a dance on the floor,
Echoes of playtime, we always adore.
In the tapestry woven, they're threads of delight,
With giggles and purrs, they fill up the night.

So here's to the moments when laughter is free,
With a purring companion, just you and me.
In a furry embrace, pure joy we trace,
Life is a treasure, with love to embrace.

Paws and Paradoxes

Furballs bounce with pure delight,
Chasing shadows in the night.
Whiskers twitch with playful glee,
Philosophy's not for me!

They nap on books, oh what a scene,
Why read when I can watch them preen?
Life's a joke they seem to know,
Paws in the air, logic can go!

Water bowls are fancy pools,
They reign as kings, and we're the fools.
Chasing tails is their big plan,
What's meaning, when they'll nap and ran?

With every pounce and every leap,
They question life while I just weep.
In warm sunbeams, they find their truth,
While I'm left searching my own youth.

The Essence of Fur

Soft and fluffy, a joy to hold,
They purr like engines, never cold.
Nine lives seem a small conceit,
In one lap, they don't retreat.

They rule the couch, a comfy throne,
Forget the world, I'm not alone.
Fur in my coffee, a daily grind,
It's the essence of what's defined.

Mysterious beings, masters of chill,
With quiet paws, they bend my will.
Meaning's just a cat's meow,
And life's a nap, I'll take a bow.

Our days are filled with silly quests,
For hidden treats, they run the tests.
In every purr, I find my muse,
Oh, the joys I cannot lose!

Catnip Reveries

In a world of catnip dreams,
They battle foes in moonlit beams.
Unraveling yarn with all their might,
In their minds, they win each fight.

Boxes seem like castles grand,
Adventures mapped across the land.
Chasing dust motes, in sudden sprints,
Philosophers? No, just little gints.

Peering out through window frames,
They judge the world and its silly games.
With one soft paw, they call my name,
As if the earth should feel the same.

In cosmic dreams, they rule the skies,
While I sit here, laughing, oh my!
What's life but treats and cozy beds?
With feline wonders filling our heads.

Solitude in a Soft Purr

A soft purr breaks the silence wide,
While I ponder, they just glide.
In sun-drenched spots, they claim their throne,
Philosophy? No, that's just my phone.

With twitching tails and sleepy eyes,
They shriek at nothing, what a surprise!
Chasing their dreams in slumber deep,
While I question why I even weep.

A subtle wiggle and playful leap,
Their antics are the joys I keep.
In every scratch and gentle rub,
Lies the meaning of our little hub.

They stretch and nap, so full of cheer,
Who needs wisdom when they're near?
In solitude, purrs echo loud,
In cuddly warmth, I'm ever proud.

www.ingramcontent.com/pod-product-compliance
Ingram Content Group UK Ltd.
Pitfield, Milton Keynes, MK11 3LW, UK
UKHW010437170125
4146UKWH00047B/222